Hello, Ev

Dot the Bird

By Howie Minsky

Dot is a bird.

Dot likes hunting.

Dot likes lily pads.

Dot likes water.

Dot likes stretching.

Dot likes grass.

Dot likes walking.

Dot likes hiding.

Dot likes worms.

Dot likes grasping.

Dot likes bending.

Dot likes eating.

Word List

bird
hunting
lily
pads
water
stretching
grass
walking
hiding
worms
grasping
bending
eating

38 Words

Dot is a bird.
Dot likes hunting.
Dot likes lily pads.
Dot likes water.
Dot likes stretching.
Dot likes grass.
Dot likes walking.
Dot likes hiding.
Dot likes worms.
Dot likes grasping.
Dot likes bending.
Dot likes eating.

Published in the United States of America by Cherry Lake Publishing
Ann Arbor, Michigan
www.cherrylakepublishing.com

Photo Credits: © Howie Minsky

Library of Congress Cataloging-in-Publication Data has been filed and is available at catalog.loc.gov

Printed in the United States of America
Corporate Graphics

CHERRY BLOSSOM PRESS